33 Mystic Notes

SEYED KOUROSH MIRTAGHI

BALBOA.
PRESS

A DIVISION OF HAY HOUSE

Balboa Press books may be ordered through booksellers or by contacting:

Balboa Press
A Division of Hay House
1663 Liberty Drive
Bloomington, IN 47403
www.balboapress.com
1 (877) 407-4847

Print information available on the last page.

ISBN: 978-1-9822-0712-0 (sc)
ISBN: 978-1-9822-0710-6 (hc)
ISBN: 978-1-9822-0711-3 (e)

Library of Congress Control Number: 2018907352

Balboa Press rev. date: 06/30/2018

Contents

Preface

A long time ago, there was a mighty merchant who dreamed while sleeping, a voice telling him to go to the town's Hammam (public bath) and watch the Bath-keeper!

This happened in two consecutive nights. Following the third night's repetition of the same dream, he went to the town's public bath, started to watch the Bath-keeper and his struggle of much trouble and toil to bring the wood from a far distance to keep furnace working all through the day with no rest.

He went closer and said: "You have a hard work in such a hot weather!"

"This too shall pass" : The Bath-keeper replied.

A year passed by and it happened again for the mighty merchant to have the same dream in his sleep. When he went to look for the Bath-keeper in the public bath. This time, he noted that his position's been upgraded to the Bath-treasurer inside the bath.

"Your work is more comfortable now." the mighty merchant said.

"This too shall pass" : The Bath-keeper replied again.

The mighty merchant had the same dream two years later and he went to the town's market after finding him not being a Bath-keeper anymore but having a huge famous shop in the main market and being famous as one of the town's Trustees.

"Greeting, how wonderful, you have grown a lot!" The mighty merchant said.

"This too shall pass!" The Bath-keeper repeated with a smile on his face.

Sometimes later the mighty merchant was invited to the town's palace for an event. Suddenly he saw the previous Bath-keeper and now being as the King in the town. He went ahead and with tribute and respect, said:

"It is my honor and I am proud to see my friend as the great King of the town!"

"This too shall pass." The King replied, repeating the gentle smile.

Mighty merchant was surprised and thinking profoundly all through the day: "What else could he want in his life?"

A few years passed, and the mighty merchant returned to the same town and decided to visit his friend where he found out that he has died recently. The merchant with sorrow went to the cemetery for his friend's tribute.

"This too shall pass." Was engraved on his Tombstone.

A few months later the cemetery was vanished by flood.

"In the Name of the Creator of Love and Hope"

It would be an honor to provide deeply from the heart a few practical words toward the self-recognition.

Although we are all seekers in this world, these writings are useful for the honest seekers of the self and truth.

English is not my native language and I still prefer using my own words and vocabularies rather than recruiting a linguistic for the purpose of bookman art.

It might not appear to be polished and professional, it nevertheless fulfils its function as a means of communication, among us.

Moving from personality toward individuality and self-recognition is certainly the basic step for man to be performed. Social laws has shaped since the very beginning of human history. Even thinking about it might not be possible!

Transcending the mind is the key, my friend!

It would be the same as entering a dance-scene for the first time.

If you are aware and present enough, all the hindrances talking to your ears through the mind will disappear.

The fear, embarrassment, ridicule, failure, and all the rest of ideas which are mostly being negative will disappear immediately. Besides, all the mind's ideas having their point of view to consider, yet somehow, your body is intelligent enough to manage and enjoy the dance. Allowing all parts of the body to function more autonomously with full awareness and presence. It is an exercise for the body.

Once you begin the dance, all the negative factors start to melt down and when you observe your body, you will note this intelligence. Indeed you literally observe the body and notice the separation of the observer and the body. This is the "Dance".

And if you watch closely enough, you will be surprised, how skilfully your body manages situations without trying to. Naturally in coping with self and surrounding; that you were not even aware of!

And if watching attentively, one notes the certain distance between the certain parts of true self, namely the body, the persona, the emotions, the observer and relations among them. In the well-formed personality of contemporary man, only a trace of these relations are present!

> *"The secret of eternity, neither Thee know nor do I,*
> *The solution to life's enigma, neither Thee know nor do I,*
> *Beneath the Veil stand the dialog of Thee and I,*
> *Removing the Veil; neither Thee remain nor do I."*

Omar Khayyam, the Master, the Poet

To find one's unique and inherent divine design urges continuous striving, of which in contemporary time viewing, it appears to go against the stream at the first glance.

But by looking with an honest eye and deeper, one will certainly find the righteous.

Honesty is the secret!

That is a mystery since it is the only way to touch the reality. Yet, it has been forgotten a long time ago and the most are engaged with their lives superficially.

The journey toward the true self requires a determined man my friend!

Within this vast beautiful world, man, with his ideas, wisdom, and philosophies, and his temptations and desires, to flowers and fruits surrounding him within the garden of life; hidden from the eyes and attentions, there is a path deep down in the garden.

This unique path is to be lived and experienced, yet, the man has to be matured and to transcend. The farther one goes in the path, the emptier it becomes, yet the higher presence of self.

This extraordinary and mysterious path, being as close as breath to the self, yet inaccessible by five senses.

A blind man in a dark summer night, just after midnight,
passing in a small alley in his town, while carrying Lantern.
He was noticed by a passer-by who by chance knew him.
"How are you, friend? What is the gain of carrying light
to you with no eyes?" The passer asked the blind man.
The blind man answered him:
"This light is for those who think they see, yet are blind,
to see me thus avoiding the crash between us two!"

Unless all the superficial attractions and temptations accessible to man drop off, he would not be able to note farther beyond his close vicinity.

The unhooking requires being in real sense and sincere, to expand the vision.

Out of hand, one tastes the truth and the adventure begins. That is the activating point. The hardness is to let go of all flowers and fruits seduction and find the road.

This is possible by inquiring through heart my friend!

Everything is transient but the essence. Seeker therefore gradually comprehends the nature of the essence and he realizes that he is a passer because he persistently remembers himself. And yet, he is the only one being able to help him.

"Awareness of momentum" is the essence of this passage. Lasting attachments cause a journey to slow down and eventually to end, while the destination itself, is of no interest to seeker.

Possession is not worthy enough to end the journey.

Man requires to develop and strengthen in all aspects. The amount of suffering depends directly on the amount of load on the back and size of the bite taken, individually.

The progression of development will accelerate significantly when one works on all parts of his life simultaneously. This allows for experiencing and learning in all centers from a single event concurrently.

Although these words might look spiritual, heroic or poetic, that is how they appear on the surface, they are not intended for that purpose though. They might appear artistic or from dreamland out of perceptions. The more artistic and dream-like they appear, the more distance is in one's journey.

But distance is not influencing the achievement my friend!

The human is by nature, a weak creature whose life is passing by. He is unable and incapable to do anything. For the man to be flourished, changing this situation, there are certain measures and moves to be performed, regardless of his personal beliefs.

The initial fact is to percept oneself in a temporary physical body.

The process of recognition and development of true self produces a path which is the result of the whole journey.

That path is full of ups and downs, a higher state of awareness, in general, is required to maintain one in the path and keep advancing.

The seeker goes patiently and quietly my friend!

He gains something from every dwelling, event, contemplation, interaction, integration, idea and he goes on with no bondage.

Man is not capable of grasping a desire and holding to it strongly, while expecting to move forward.

Time is limited to forms and it requires you to avoid unnecessary disruption.

Youth is passing by, show me the one appreciating it!

Wisdom says no attachments, enjoy the taste with the tip of your finger, be thankful and let it go with appreciation.

Watchful acknowledgment of the transient physical world is a key to moving forward.

The initial step is to remove the boundaries, re-adjust, and adapt oneself to its most possible natural state of being.

The prerequisite to this step is recognition of the whole being and the true self.

Welcoming full of love and awareness blissfully, is the state to be attained in the path.

It appears as much as a lifetime fulfilment.

The secret is always to remain seeker my friend!

Despite this all, time is not an important factor to determine the length of the journey. The more degree of purity and sincerity, the more achievements are.

A religious man follows instructions and seeker follows the heart. A truly religious man eventually becomes a seeker.

People all indeed are seekers, the difference is in the degree of one's awareness of the fact.

One goes with the instructions, another with heart.
Oceanic heart flaming with love is the key!

To move; man requires to enter the field and perceive the truth. That is how reality is being created and the man has the power to influence it and eventually become a creator oneself.

To become the highest, you need to do all by yourself.

When reading, it requires the mind to be free from outside world. Drop it all, allow your heart to be present.

Dive deeply with the courage to this void, touching the words and senses one by one with depth. It permits the advancement.

Don't take these words as advices my friend!

They only have a point to note, easing the comprehension of the self and the world. That is all. While advice, results in habits.

Words coming from the heart are true, courageous, hermetic and melodious, and when they produce action directly, it manifests and shines!

Next time when you see a row of ants engaged with their busy lives, observe them closely and note the beauty of their harmonious movement, purposefully with designed actions.

Sitting long enough you may go beyond it, sometimes, a single lost ant wandering around in another world than the rest, in different harmony.

More perceptible and natural as if there is no winter to come. With no fear of life or future!

Sometimes I wonder how this ant could share his world with the rest of his colony. From the Workers through the Queen!

"Where is the One, making me drunk, wineless?
And where is the One, separating my soul and heart, Bodyless?

The One who I oath to, not to drink anymore, but to its Glory!
The One, making me break my oath and repentance!
Where is the One?"

Rumi the Master, the Poet

Another requirement for Seeker is to encounter all thoughts and emotions of any nature.

The use of language is limited quantitatively and qualitatively due to the complexity of the word's meanings and variation of personal experiences and points of views.

Regardless of how rich one's knowledge is, its use is limited.

In contemporary time also, the words are powerless, shallow and subject to abuse.

The mind itself is the product of this world. Therefore, it is unable to realize and comprehend the reality beyond itself. It is wise to use it only when needed. To know when it is needed, one requires to cease the conversations within.

Initially, physical and emotional ways of communications require being integrated into the talkative language deeply, to give it a soul, a depth, and a base for a higher dimension.

Simplicity and *Patience* are the secrets my friend!

A certain amount of awareness and consciousness are required for self-recognition which is higher than values in the norm of society in both amount and quality.

To gain and expand consciousness, it is to be noted first and gradually grown and developed by self-observation.

The love, mysteriously, creates the optimal conditions for it all! It guides through the way known and unknown harmoniously.

When this process is performed purely through the heart with the effect of love radiance covering everything, it transforms one's life immediately!

"Love" is beyond emotional experiences. It is the most abundant power!

To reach to this point one requires being ready. The readiness of body, mind, and soul laboring works to do.

Suffering and austerity are not the prices to be paid for it. But it is an experience resulting from reactivation of various parts of the true self from its dormant form. The reason for dormant state is because of gradual ignorance through the time.

It requires a higher amount of energy for keeping one inside the way. This will be acquired in a gradual way. Hence the words are limited to convince the mind but if one remains patient and persistent in the path, one would gradually and eventually taste the truth and regain the fire inside flaming.

Every man has entered to this world for a piece of unique work to complete. Self-recognition is prior to all kind of labors my friend!

If you find the path, everything sits where it belongs to, effortlessly. In that states "I" dissolves while the body, mind and soul act individually and yet as One harmoniously. Acceptance ensures the way.

These all require a higher state of being achieved and in lower states, it is highly challenging to keep the impetus toward it.

Trust is the key!

It is not the question of how one approves it, but how one is ready and present to face, deal and accept the truth.

One might live the whole life entirely and die without even noting the truth. Whether you will become aware of it and find it also depends on the efforts toward it, beside other factors.

The question of the benefit of the path is to be discovered by man himself. Of course when maturing sufficiently individually.

Unfortunately, the criteria at the current age are based on unimportant and worthless matters, producing stagnation of individual. In addition there is a "competition factor". Although the one to blame is the man himself for it, it is contemporary style of slavery of the individual.

For some, there is a long grey desert and wilderness beforehand realizing the way.

Having the quality of seeker with great flexibility and readiness for change, is the solution.

You are the only one in your infinite world, look for yourself to find your world my friend!

One should be fully ready for the journey. One should be determined.

In the ocean, on a piece of wood, it is vain to row!

Words and sayings are infinite, they come out of the mouth, and they are attractive. The substance is, however, the action created by the true self. Unless the man acts and creates, it is futile, no matter how significant and major the impressions are.

Sun is shining equally to all around and depending on the positions, it is received differently. For man, this fact is not affecting the quality but the variety of the path. But if man allows and trusts his heart to be the shipmaster, then he is kept in the way spontaneously.

Prior to it, one should find the essence and the true self thus to become a creator. At the same time, one should respect others and try to learn from all around as much as possible.

It appears as a metaphor, yet it is true my friend!

There is a fire inside! Its flame being of love and light. It is covered with a layer of ash making it flicker. It requires a wind to remove the ash and let the fire blaze again.

Cease the conversations to unfold the fire inside!

Writings are not the best way of trade to sell the words in this era. But being sincere enough, the man listening by his heart finds it just right and sufficient. It is not an easy treasure!

The matter of sociality of man-being as a species is a subject to be asked not by intellectuals, scientists or thinkers but by every single individual, in a natural and honest way, to identify the best way of living for herself/himself.

The man, however, should become a true "Man" before asking this question from the self. It requires to obtain the right answer and choose the right way.

On the surface, it does not matter but in profound, it should be reviewed by everyone. This does not relate to the concept of philanthropy.

The quantitative size of the society compatible with the nature of man for being fully grown varies with considering different conditions for an individual. They are namely the age, and the degree of self-recognition attained by the individual, the environment of society and so on. But in higher numbers, chaos is produced.

Hence the formation of masters and disciples, to solve this hindrance, since very old ages naturally.

The streets are full of people and by observing them, their ideas and conversations closely, one would find the worthless matters, are being the top objects of communication, willingly or not; regardless of what is being ideal or right. As if in a deep sleep!

The fact is involvement and relation to the surrounding living conditions, and superficial expansion of namely society of people, who have nothing in common in a real sense, except the worldly desires, all competing in a polite and modern way. But rarely desires originate from all parts of man and the true self.

These relations are held by the factors, originating by instincts, rather than man's true position in the universe.

There are various distances available for the man in a community; from the closest between friends and family counterpointing the opposite end in the society, and the use of language and speaking as a tool for communication would be superficial toward the latter before knowing the self.

Irrespective of how detailed and logic are the objects of conversation, the outcome and the amount of communication, interaction is variable and usually on the lower side.

The unequal degree of active individualities present, is the main reasons behind it.

Discipline is the mystery my friend!

It is significant to optimize the conditions throughout the way. To benefit most, read by your heart silently and perceive every word, vividly.

Developing and growing the insight.

Every word has only one meaning. Experience the words with the right meaning.

Love is the remedy! Let your heart thrill the way.

There are certain requirements:

- To be a seeker
- Discipline

- Honesty
- Patience

The Discipline is a temporary measure.

I use my heart for communication, allow the same from your side to be established, grown and become the way of communication onward and eventually your way of living.

I already love you, and I already trust you my friend.

Unfolded the love and passion, they are two inseparable characters and power.

Love is the nature and force behind.

Passion is formed within a short time interval while love requires longer term for its complete development.

One should become thirsty to look for the water; realization to know oneself is performed by close self-observation.

The miracle is how to lead and activate one to have the thirst.

The appropriate observation allows awareness and attention to watch the self closely and continuously while searching for water. This, in turn, reveals the strong areas for the seeker to lean on, and the deficits to be worked on.

Discipline requires to be strict and on physical, mental and emotional dimensions and in a sincere way.

Honesty is the true state of being of complete man which requires to be regained.

Passion is power coming from one's essence. It exists at various levels of intensity. It expresses itself either through a gradual way of self-recognition process or as a sudden matter.

Seeker is produced in such a way, where one's reality and the world become overwhelmed. Love being the power nourishing it all.

In any case if you are eager and passionate, it requires nourishment and looking after enough continuously and actively; otherwise, it returns to the dormant state.

Man's trust has been faded slowly throughout his existence and state of *Presence* has been dropped to the state of *being*.

The sense of responsibility has been taken away slowly; once the child is born, consciously or not the child becomes an actor of life.

And once the child is grown, the same criteria and rules of parents and society become his and by the time the child has noticed it, he is physically a grown adult and likely, on the second half of the life.

It requires regaining the trust my friend!

Patience is developed when the cause for hurry is identified and dealt with; that is how the patience, can be naturally formed and experienced.

Patience is a positive and active phenomena.

Patience is purposefully and strategically being ready and waiting for what is expected and what is not!

On patience; it is not slowing down the passage of time, but control of self in the passage through the time, to transcend beyond it.

Self-centering and accessing within are the secrets!

Life is the battle scene of the mind and the heart; I wish you to tame this rogue horse my friend.

It has been quoted about Bayazid Bastami, the great Sufi master:
Once he was in solitude, he spoke the word: "I glorify what is greatest!"

"Such a word came into your language": Disciples
told him when he came around.
Bayazid said:
"Woe to you and woe to me! You are all in
deep sleep, I am in deep sleep!

Tear me to pieces if such worlds appear again in my language,
and he then armed them with knives and daggers."
It happened the other night once again, he spoke the words of the
same nature. When disciples determined to kill him, suddenly
the house was accumulated with "Bayazid" everywhere!
All the bricks of the house were out, cut and sliced in
disciples attempt to kill the Master, with no hit being able
to touch Bayazid. A few hours later when the disciples
were exhausted and convinced of the immortality of the
Master, when he came around sitting in his adytum.
The disciples gathered around him and told the story, and he said:
"This is the Bayazid that you are seeing right now, I'm
not sure whom you where confronting therewith."

Life is indeed a journey toward absolute which requires bodily, mentally and emotional preparation and development rather than speechifying the details and stick on surface.

Higher measure of energies are required, shifting the energy expenditure from inessential matters to substantial labors of life.

All the efforts are to be focused on reaching the platform of sufficient self-recognition with complete awareness and presence. That is the point where the life gets the real meaning my friend!

And onward achievement is to be explored and created individually.

That is the re-birth of man.

There will be no self to create anymore, and there will be no soul to claim neither. There will be just the truth; accessible continuously.

To achieve this, a determined and surrendered man with a courageous and compassionate heart is required.

These words require contemplation my friend!

These are not to be taught, but experienced impartially.

Beforehand it requires recognizing and indwelling Love entirely and knowing its customs and traditions thoroughly.

The path is waiting for all to be completed, the grave is to discover it early enough in one's lifetime, to be able to advance sufficiently!
This journey gradually causes translocation of the center of self from head to the heart.
Considering the current era, this transformation produces suffering for most, but with the development of insight and practice, it disappears.

The truth is as if rope walking, and the Seeker is the ropewalker, attentive and present continuously with the lucid mind in equilibrium with the surrounding. Experiencing the truth with no attachment to the moment gone, nor to the next one to come.
How far one would go and how close one would get to it, depends on persistence and passion.
A brave heart is the clue!

The length of the exercises for practices varies from days to months depending on the person.
Exercises require mastering with the full depth rather than formation of an advice in the head! That is the accumulation of ego-satisfying knowledge with minimal real effect, which is the habit of man in contemporary.

Body, mind, and heart all require being prepared, trained and developed my friend!

Love

*"The secret of Love should not be spoken to all.
Those who are not freed from the self and those, whose
hearts, have not been glorified with beloved lights yet.
How could they realize the position of love without
having the required capacity for it?*

*Although they appear as wise and scholar, mighty or great
religious man, the secret must be shared with trusting
people only, and those luminous with beloved lights."*

Jaami, the Master, the Poet

In the path of love whatever may come, is welcomed by heart my friend!

Love is the most abundant and creative power in existence. The heart works as the center of divinity in man, listening by heart you will feel butterflies in the stomach. That is just like the unique sinking effect in the gut while being in a vehicle driving down a dip in the road.

That is the moment to focus!

17

Next time, witness the thrill and notice the port opening just in that specific moment.

That port is the mystery!

To produce such a continuous state, it requires higher levels of energy flow, concentration and awareness.

The stream of love is not affected by beloved properties, but by the amount of love radiating from the lover.

Try to thread a needle passionately by your heart and compare it with ordinary mechanical action, alternatively.

See the differences.

To have a full sense of love it requires the heart being functional and dissolving the boundary of self and outside world.

Allow the true love to enter your life fully.

Living in and being in touch with nature and simplicity in lifestyle would allow this activation to happen smoothly.

Gradually one notice the changes, it seems that things happening are different, but just right.

Practice is necessary for all forms of activities.

Love is the force of living, love makes the *Dance*!

Allow honest love to nourish your life and your whole presence continuously.

Be thankful and patient my friend.

Awareness

"In the distant days, in the city of Baghdad, there lived a rich man by the wealth of his father's inheritance.

He was very light-minded, voluptuous, and pleasure-loving. He was famous for his prodigality and having feasts and entertainments, wasting away his wealth.

Soon his money was over, he became poor and indigent, not even having food to eat, no friends stayed with him neither.

Nothing left for him, he decided to pray days and nights, for granting him and may God have mercy upon him and save him.

Days were passing, and he continued to pray, till one late midnight as he was praying since early hours of morning, he fell asleep. In a dream, a voice told him: "Hey you, go to Egypt to such city, street, and such house, there is a treasure for you!"

The man jumped from his bed and presumed his dream as true. Two days later he left Baghdad for Egypt and within few days finally he got to the right city, the street, and the right house. But he was tired and hungry, and as no money was left for him, he decided to beg people. But he felt embarrassed, he waited for night to come, so no one could see his face.

By night's arrival however, there was no one outside already, to beg from.

Out of nowhere a night guard caught him from behind and started to beat him all-over, all he could do was screaming.

After being beaten hip-and-thigh, he begged the guard to give him a chance to justify himself. Then he told the guard whole story over.

The night guard laughed loudly and said:

"You idiot! I keep having a dream for many years about a hidden treasure in Baghdad in such street and such house, but I never even thought of going to Baghdad for it!"

But, when the man noted that the treasure address given by guard was his own house, he said goodbye quietly to him, and the guard also let him go.

Then, the man immediately returned to Baghdad and found the treasure in the hidden place in the house and onward he used the wealth appropriately.

From Masnavi, by Rumi, the Master, the Poet

Results of your actions depend on the amount of your own knowledge, wisdom, and awareness integrated together simultaneously, plus the quality of action produced.

Man is composed of centers of interactions between the external stimuli and internal receptive being.

The awareness is the key!

The external stimuli are from obvious sources with different outcomes and imperceptible sources with the indirect result, beyond the comprehension of logic mind.

The forces inside are originated or saved from without.

Man requires to control the powers and manifest it as much as in his hand, respectively to obtain the desired actions.

Five sensory organs and mind are main responsible devices to produce awareness initially which require to be worked on.

At the contemporary time these organs, and mainly of the visual sense, are either used superficially, overused or abused, hence the minimal results.

Mind functions to sense the unreachable beyond the visual range, hence the correct knowledge and wisdom are to be obtained in order to have an appropriate action and result.

The true knowledge of life, by man, is acquired only by the individual my friend!

Self-observation is the efficient way to intensify and expand the awareness.

Knowledge acquired mentally, should be digested by all parts of being including body and soul, to create a harmonious and desired reaction.

With right actions and pieces of training, the consciousness and awareness expands progressively.

Self-observation requires tremendous amount of energy, effort and strive requiring continuous practice and patience.

Mind quietude is the basic prerequisite and an effective exercise to be performed. Cease the inside conversation!

It should be practiced on 'daily basis' and as routine if not began already.

The good training for observation would be having an imaginary camera or an imaginary eye above once head at all-time continuously and watch!

At the beginning the awareness produced will be interruptive, by time it becomes continuous. The results would be available instantly following this exercise.

Adjust this imaginary camera or eye to yourself in various distances above the head depending on field for the observation and one's consciousness size. It might be just above the head to focus on the self and a certain action being performed, or it might go higher to cover a small area and few people or subjects, or it might even go to cover entire city, continent or the earth and beyond.

Be fully aware of the camera/eye always throughout the day and night.

Be aware of communications, interactions, gestures, mimics, cravings, and needs. The initial aim is to obtain a complete *self-observation*.

At night time before going to sleep review your actions physically, mentally and emotionally utterly, beginning in revise mode, from most recent toward the first thing which was done in the morning.

In the morning note your dreams, thoughts or actions during the night gone.

Be an honest observer!

Practice it until you are aware of yourself on the momentum perpetually, with no requirement to review your actions at night time.

Listen by heart

"Heart's ear and Heart's eye, are other than these senses,
Mind's ear, Suspicion's eye, both belong to poor Me!

Word of 'Compulsion', has inbred the Impatience in Love,
If not in Love, you are the imprisoner of 'Compulsion'!

Rumi, the Master, the Poet"

There are higher senses beyond physical ones.

Ignorance at contemporary era, is the result of dormant states of these senses!

Love and surrender are the keys!

Listening by one's heart requires dedication and presence compassionately to the object.

For an instant, the object becomes part of the self.

The heart is a fair device for communications. It utilizes all inputs known and unknown to man, establishing connection in a natural way.

Improving the quality of heart sensation is a gradual process and time consuming for an ordinary man. Interaction through heart with others and animal, accelerates the process.

The Impetus

"Thou created the night... I made the lamp;
Thou created the clay... I made the cup.

The desert, mounts and the meadow, Thou created;
The road, rosaries and the garden... I made.

I am the one, making mirror out of stone!
I am the one, making drink out of poison!

Iqbal Lahori, the Master, the Poet"

As an organic being, the receptivity is the nature of man and throughout life, he receives an infinite number of incentives. Occasionally they will be influential enough and remembered to produce a motivation and change for a certain time.

Most of the excitations are not noted. Motivations can affect the man's action in life.

By observation of this receptivity, actions and reactions produce enduring of various measures depending on the completeness of individuality which may results in a conscious selection of right receptions, thus the actions. By expansion of this observation, it empowers the man to see and access beyond the ordinary world.

Patience is the key and the door to solve the puzzle. Save your energy my friend!

Being an early bird is the character of Seeker and a sign of prosperity. Going for a walk every other day, preferably somewhere in nature will help to build this useful habit.

When walking, try to focus your vision on an object on the horizon and keep your eyes there continuously through the walk. Trust your legs and body. Allow them to walk by themselves, rather than through the mind. Your body is intelligent enough to manage its functions.

Be alert and aware of around by the peripheral vision and other senses.

You will be master of this walk once you are able to go up and down hills without focusing on your walking process through the mind.

Correct your diet, increase your water intake and go to bed early.

World of Temptations

Luqman the Wise, out of hand spoke with his son:
"Son, today, I give you three advices for your prosperity.
First, try to eat the best food in the world!
Second, sleep in the best bed in the world!
And third, live in the best castles and houses in the world!"

"O father, you know that we are a poor family." Son said.
Luqman the Wise replied:
"If you eat less and a little later than usual time when the hunger
appears, then whatever you eat, it tastes like the best food in the world!
If you work a bit more and sleep less, wherever you sleep,
it feels like sleeping in the best bed in the world!
And if you would be compassionate with people and indwell yourself
in their heart, then the best houses in the world would be yours!"

Lust, power, wealth, fame and name, they are all pleasing and mellow, but, they are not all in this world. Although they are eye-catching, they should not make eyes blind. And mind plays the major role in stagnation.

The situations, good or evil, all require to be percipient and touched individually.

Or it can be comprehended by one's insight with no need for its physical experience.

The latter way would be suitable for most of the situations and it is of high value considering limitation of time for man. But the insight is to be developed initially.

Try asking few elderly people for the advice, regarding things they would not have done in past if they could, and more, and listen by your heart to their answers my friend!

Find the attractions beyond the five senses.

Careful self-observation, living simply with gratitude and acceptance of reality are the secrets!

Experience, appreciate its joy, find and accept facts and let it go.

By expansion of the consciousness, one would notice higher desires in real sense gradually. It is the road to the dreamland.

Drop the habit of watching TV and minimize the digital world my friend!

It will substantially expand and deepen the insight.

It also helps to strengthen and to maintain the essence presence and a higher awareness of self.

Preparation

An explorer traveled a far distance to a small remote
village in the mountain to visit a famous ascetic.
When he arrived, noted that Ascetic's room was full
of books and there was nothing else except a desk and
couch. And this dialogue between two took place:
The Explorer: "Where is your household?"

The Master asked: "Where are yours?"

The Explorer: "I am a traveler here."

"Me too!"
Ascetic replied."

It is all about attachments. From air to food, pain to comfort,
fantasy to lust, sugar to drugs and from powers to Gods.

They have taken a long time to form and grow through social life
generation to generation. They are the background of whole man's
action and behavior.

The hardship is to become aware of these dependencies by the individual, the rest of the story is an illusion, despite its complexity, it simply disappears.

Observation and discipline are the mysteries my friend!

The more you know about yourself, the more you realize what is really required to be rectified.

The attachments are of physical, emotional, and psychological.

To identify them it requires honesty.

Observe attachments invading the loneliness, allow them to unfold completely while watching.

Once identified then deal with them one by one, going to its depth and undoing the knot. If needed with acceptance and forgiveness my friend!

The true liberation occurs with full awareness, producing satisfactory outcomes, otherwise, it would become repressed, hidden and looking for an opportunity to return.

Use natural foods and drink. Know your body, feel it, love it.

Observe your various feelings and their origins sincerely.

Observe your sexual life attentively. There is a gross difference in between social, personal and individual comprehension of this word.

They require time and attention to be corrected.

If not abused, sex is a creative power my friend!

Observe your body, feelings, and thoughts separately and follow their interactions among them triggered by that action, feeling or thought.

Allow the purest intent to be present.

While walking, be fully alert of all your surroundings.

Increase your non-visual alertness by other senses and your mind. This is done effortlessly when fully present,

One can be as aware of events out of the sight as those within the visual field.

Master in all senses thoughtlessly. Remember the Dance my friend!

Let the gratitude be flourished and absorbed into your core warmly.

Axiom of Love

Once upon a time, there was a man in love.
He used to cross a sea, every night to meet his beloved. Even
the roaring waves of the sea were not able to stop him.
Friends and acquaintances always blamed him for it, but the young
man never listened to them. The meeting with beloved was motive,
powerful enough to ease the hardships and afflictions on his way.

One night just like the others, when he saw his
beloved, he suddenly wondered with surprise:
"Why have you got a spot on your face?"

"I had this spot since the first day we met, and I wonder
how you did not notice that before!" Beloved answered.

"True, I never noted that before. The lover said."
And the conversation continued:

"What is the scar on that corner of your face?"

"I had this scar since my childhood and I am
surprised how you have not seen it!"

31

"Not indeed, never noted that before."

"What's happened to your front tooth? It looks broken."

"It happened when I was a kid..."

*And the conversation goes on the same way with
more complains and fuss by the lover.
They stayed together till the dawn and as previous
nights the lover prepared to go back.*

The beloved said: "Don't go tonight, the sea is stormy!"

*"The sea has been much worse, and it could not stop me
dear, it can't hinder me!" The lover man replied.*

*And the beloved answered:
"At that time, you were in love and the love was rescuing you. This
time, I don't see the love, but the lust only. Don't go back tonight!"*

*The lover did not stay despite all persistency.
He was drowned in the storm whilst crossing back the sea.*

From Masnavi, by Rumi, the Master, the Poet

Next time when you notice a moth nearby a fire, watch it
carefully, the joyful whirling of it.
Sight the story behind the scene my friend!

The mind is to be absent there for moth.
First the light is noted in distance.
By getting closer to the source of light, then the love enters the
game directly, with light, beauty, and warmth. The cheerful dance
is the results.

If fortunate enough, you might see also the rare final step of unifying of the lover and the beloved one, burning up the moth inside the fire.

Watch the whole process carefully. The intoxication of love, such actions can only be originated directly from the heart.
Love is an intelligent power in existence.
Love and compassion originate from the self outwardly to the external world, dissolving of lover and beloved in love.

But the first one to be loved is the self my friend!
That is the axiom of love.
With loving oneself outwardly, the subject and object become one, one of the results is insight's transcendence.
Quietly and present!

Know your body, communicate with it, and be aware of self-continuity.
Every single cell, tissue, and organ of your body is intelligent. Bring the consciousness to all parts of your body.
Every single cell of you has been adjusted according to its receptivity to the external world.
See them separately one by one and notice the adaptations, see the whole functional frame of your body.
Master the love axiom by observation my friend.

You will need a healthy body, mind, and heart through the life and it will be gradually regained by Seeker.
The heart is far more sagacious than the logic mind. *Fear* can function through the mind, not the heart! The mind is the product of world while the love its producer.
If one desires deep from the heart, the self will adopt with one's desires and dreams. Doing the same wish by the mind dominancy is the simple repetition of already existing manifestations in the world!

Allow the heart to enjoy your breath, food, drink, pain, happiness, sorrow, fear, hot and cold, or simply let it feel all situations in your life. Know that all situations are available on the table.

Mind functions simply in dealing with surrounding world.

The fire is the cause of attraction, the mind only assists moving throughout the way.

Both are right, the view of points, are to be noted.

The Will

"*If I am Good and if Evil,*

You go and be Yourself!"

Hafez, the Tongue of Mystery

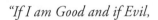

By correcting the language of think and talk, every word gets more depth and precise meaning approaching the truth.

Wish, will, dream, desire, and passion, although, they originate from the same source, yet they differ in quantities and qualities.

The major element, playing role in forming and differentiating them is the magnitude of the consciousness present.

By reviewing previous wishes in whole life since childhood honestly, one can notice the fact of relativity and transientness of the successes and satisfactions obtained. Note also the differences in qualities and the achievements.

Wishes arising in younger ages and childhood are more originating from one's essence and heart.

Find out those originating from the person and those from the individual, compare them impartially.

The higher presence of essence creates more complexity of the will. It is when the body, mind, and heart are contributing to that decision to be made.

The different dimensions and corners are considered by different parts, separately and together. The mind is not the commander, but the coordinator!

The intention is a conscious process.

Common desires in man are usually short termed and are arising from instinct centers. They depend on surrounding vicinities.

A firm intention moves a mountain if there are enough passion, love, and determination involved!

Observing the people of different ages and their behaviors, gestures, psyches, the ways of talk, actions and interactions closely, one gets the eye to see their wishes, desires, intentions and wills.

Find the one who is free from the desires my friend!

Sincerity is the key!

Disarming the Ego

In ancient times, a famous King went to see a Hermit. When the King entered, the Master was busy whilst reading a book, he did not turn his head up, nor did he humble the King. The King, full of anger told him:
"Do you know who I am?
I am that mighty King who killed such jerk and punished hard such disobedient. I was victorious in such famous war..."

The Master laughed and said:
"I am mightier than you are, because I have been victorious to one who you are still captive in his cruel hands."

"Who is that??" King asked astonishingly.

Master replied:
"That is the Ego. I have already killed mine, but you are still a captive to your ego, you would not want me to prostrate on soil and admire a man just like me unless you were a slave to your ego!"

After listening to it all, the King was sorry and kept his head down.

To begin moving forward consciously and steadily the first requirement is to know the true self.

Complete development of senses, powers and emotions is a prerequisite.

Facing the reality and accepting the truth is the element to be confronted fearlessly.

The same way as a child starts to walk, exploring the surrounding, the parents support although useful, but it is limited, the decision for standing up and walking is to be discovered and asked by the child alone, either the reason behind this decision is hunger, thirst or curiosity it is to be made by child and not the parents.

The Thirst to walk!

The similar scenario is also in the personal and individual criteria for decisions and actions required for man.

The more individuality involved, the more advancements are achieved.

To become the true self, it requires being nobody my friend!

The gradual growth of individuality, happens by exercises with focusing on man's essence presence.

While walking, avoid looking directly at people's eyes, not as an act of ignorance, one is still aware and conscious of surrounding without direct vision. This will coordinate the different parts and balance the sensory organs involvement.

By mastering this exercise, one will realize the increase of attraction from the external world toward one self.

That is where one becomes down to earth!

About the Honesty

*A Master was speaking for his disciples, he suddenly began
telling a funny story, and everybody was laughing loudly.
After a few moments, he repeated the same joke
and this time, few audiences laughed at it.
He repeated it in a few seconds again, and
no one laughed on this occasion.*

The Master smiled and said:
*"When you can't laugh constantly to the same matter; why are
you crying repeatedly for the same and similar matters then?"*

Honesty is the natural state of being effortlessly in equilibrium, within and without.

Harmony, respect, gratitude, and acceptance are the main factors in determining the quality of impartiality.

It is regained when these factors are developed. The peak of development occurs in total harmony.

This is the only true state available, other states are a combination of some role-playing acts and states induced by the ego.

The direction opposite to honesty leads to cowardice. Avoid it my friend!

Sincerity is the only act in accordance with truth.

It leads to prosperity and man's perfection.

Honesty in its nature spontaneously protects one from performing inappropriate conducts, it leads to immunity against lying, envy, vanity, ambition, hatred and many other false states.

It is the natural state of happiness!

Courageousness is the key!

Sincerity requires continuous development.

To be present continually, requires the appreciation of external realities of any form perpetually.

Honesty is the character allowing seeker to be kept in the path.

By developing sincerity, it will become a growing core to the true self, which indeed it has been there always but ignored. When certain measure of its development is reached and continues, it represents the true features of the self. It will be attracted by others most as if having a sense of magic, seeing themselves within you.

You become a pattern for the world!

With this great progression, one can actively start self-correction reliably with imminent results.

Honesty is from the same substance as the truth.

It provides external and internal stability.

The self, the dearest ones, people in street, an animal or an object, watch them all with the sincerity my friend!

Indeed, the feeling of equality is to be perceived by the observer not from the sender. And man is only a relative receptor. This journey will induce and increase the stability of this receptor!

Animals are examples to be observed. Seeing them as a complete being, similar, just like a man. Feeling their presence and their response, all expressing their "areness"!

Watch everything with an honest eye.

Note the impartiality between positive and negative.

Neutral state is nearest to the center and the most stable state of natural equilibrium.

Live more and more in an honest way my friend!

On Surrendering

"It's been quoted that a master entered a collective.
The people there, all knew him well and
requested him for an exhortation.

The Master accepted.
After a short while, when all eyes were looking at him,
Then the Master began to talk:
"O people… Stand up those who know they will
live and not die till the midnight."

No one got up.

Then he said:
"Now, step up, those of you who are ready to die!"

No one got up neither.
And then the Master said:

"How wondrous!
You are not sure of your life and nor ready to go!"

The real masters are not seen easily, they surrender through their heart and they have given up all the name and fame.

Letting it go with acceptance is the clue.

Nature gives this power to those who have the capacity to use it my friend!

By surrendering, Fear disappears completely and the true nature of the world become visible to the seeker. By gaining its power, one becomes the master of herself/himself. The world becomes bright and in full expression.

In the path, by the time man gains a power, he simultaneously loses the interest in it, hence the way of abusing the power is lost too. Increase your capacities and save the powers!

Imagine you live in a flying airplane at all time.

No wonder the pilots are down to earth, tolerant and accepting people my friend!

Your thoughts, emotions, and actions are primarily derived from the essence and you appear and become conscientious. The truth of physical death and acceptance of life as it is, are placed very close and in touch at all time.

It is difficult to think about the death since it encounters once only and as the final scene, but the watchful presence and the insight brings also other options on the table.

Relations

It's been said a lot about the first meeting between Shams Tabrizi(the Master) and Mowlana (the Rumi), some belief as two lovers, and some as two beloveds.

Shams was an uprising and a restless soul who left his home and country, looking for someone of the same nature as himself, and he was constantly on a trip to the point where soon, he was nicknamed as "Shams the flying bird".

Shams says about his own state:
"I was looking for someone to make him my patron, and then 'Rumi' came about, where I turned to be lulled by myself!"

One day Shams enters Rumi's Assembly for the first time. Rumi was surrounded by several books whilst Shams asked him: "What are these books?"

"Controversy," Rumi replied.

"What are you going to do with them?" Shams asked,
and he immediately took the books and dropped
them all in the nearby water fountain.

"What did you just do Darvish? Some of these books
were presents from my father and they were unique
versions!" Rumi said with a sad impression.

Shams draws the books one by one back from the bed of water
with no soaking effect on them and all completely dry!

"What is the secret?" By watching it, Rumi wondered.

And Shams replied: "That is the taste of presence
and love that you are not aware of!"

This instantly alters Rumi's state to madness transiently
and eventually causing him a rebirth.
He left his lessons, discussions, and assemblies behind
and started to follow Shams, days and nights. Their
relation later goes even beyond the devotion.

It has been said that Shams was not literate while
Rumi was a senior educated person.

Especially, in contemporary times, the bargain is the basic rule for any other kind of relationship. Where there is a bargain, "better and worse" there will appear!

Popular items of this trades include wealth, lust, power, name and fame.

Trade language has numerous dialects of the same language. Don't be deceived by the flippancy my friend!

There are milliards of people in the world and all of them think they are right just right now!

The depth, the insight make the differences!
For Seeker, true relation is based on love and honesty.

Disciple gains treasure of an age out of a master; master observes himself in his disciple. This is the secret to be witnessed individually!

Difficult to find an honest friend, the easier way is to raise the sincerity in our relations.

By observing the relations of any nature sincerely, and in the relations, replacing the trades with love.

Remaining inside the path long enough will develop this sense and makes the true relation to occur.

The path

It's been quoted about the 'Attar of Nishapur', the Mystic and Poet, who was an apothecary originally, one day busy in his store with the clients, a beggar entered his store and asked him for help several times while Attar was trying to ignore him.

"Oh you, Boss, how do you want to give up your life when dying, with such attitude?"
The beggar said.

"The same way as you do." Attar replied.

-"Really like me?"

-"Yes..."

The beggar lies down placing his wooden bowl beneath his head and after a short whisper, he dies!

Attar was shocked by watching it.

He left the store and never returned.

Soon he became a disciple to one of the famous masters of his time.

There is a unique path for every single man. It resembles a twisted road on a mount toward the summit.

There are certain checkpoints on the way. They will be realized by reaching them.

Seeker requires to be ready completely and equipped for the journey my friend!

By advancing the path, purification occurs spontaneously.

The various ways toward the summit starting at the bottom, gradually merge together.

The higher on the path, the lesser become the tributes, and fewer seekers are left!

The higher one goes, lonelier one becomes producing anxiety. But by more awareness. Seeker, simultaneously realizes that he has been always alone!

The real friendship begins here when the vision is further unfolded. At this level the real values of man himself and the friendship become obvious.

The higher one goes, the fewer faces are left for the ego to keep one busy, yet although less frequent, but the stronger susceptibility to come out of the path.

One requires being an attentive observer at all time my friend!

Sometimes, man becomes aware of repeating similar actions or behaviors in his life within certain intervals, which are being evolved by time, to a nicer and cleverer actions. That is just a false upgrade of previous habit. A trick by mind!

It is due to incomplete liberations from previous attachments, unresolved certain obstacle or deficient purification.

Seeker requires reviewing oneself or looking for help constantly to correct the situation and find her/his flaws.

There are also shortcuts available, leading to bypass one or few turns of the twisted path.

Gratitude and love are the secrets.

Eliminate the causes of false fear my friend!

Avoid ignorance, the attachment requires to be released. They need attention.

On the top of the summit, no matter how many reach there, there is a place only for one: *The True Man*!

The Emotions

"A word, more pleasant than the sound of love, naught I heard;

The only great token lasting in this 'Revolving Dome'

Hafez, the Tongue of Mystery"

Emotions are the complex form of perceptions.

They are felt as a result of the soul, heart, and body interactions with outside world.

Emotions are channels through which the combined various powers will be released and expressed.

Hope, love, fear, anger, lust, anxiety, happiness and grief are examples of streams of powers participating in the formation of emotion.

Their degree of contribution varies depending on the individual and the content of each part involved in forming the emotion. There are visible and invisible emotions. All these factors contribute in the manifestation of reaction produced. Watching them carefully will lead to realizing the essence and nature of the emotions. Nowadays this is an almost intact field of knowledge to discover my friend!

The power streams require to be restrained and not suppressed, which in return the power itself would become available to use appropriately and move forward.

By gradual training, one can reserve, store and take control of the powers.

It is useful to know that the streams although combined forms, but are produced with the dominance of a single source of a current.

Mindful observation is the key my friend!

With the help of self-observation, one can note these streams and their centers and gradually begins to restrain the streams.

Art and morality are the by-products of emotional developments.

The relations between body, mind and soul, at the current time, are at the minimal levels. Knowing the emotions fully improves substantially the communication between the aforementioned components.

Stop the inner conversation for a better observation of the Emotions my friend!

The Knowledge

*Al-Ghazali, the great Mystic, and theologian left his town (Tous)
and family at youth and moved to the city of Nishapur where being
famous at the time as the House of Science, to continue his education.
For many years, he earned knowledge and pearls of
wisdom toward the perfection and maturity from
different masters, scholars, and pundits.*

*Al-Ghazali used to make notes from the learned hints and always
made regular booklets and hand-outs to keep his knowledge
handy, hence not forgetting them. He loved his writings and hand-
outs and cared for them with love, whole through these years.*

*When he decided to return to his country after many
years, he lined his hand-outs up carefully in a big
traveling bag and began his trip with a Caravan.
Perchance, the Caravan was confronted with a
group of thieves and bandits in its way.
The thieves stopped the Caravan and begin to
seize the properties of all passengers.*

*Eventually, it was Al-Ghazali's turn and the thieves were
attracted to his big bag, as they touched his bag…
Al-Ghazali began to beg and moan, asking them: "Take
whatever you want from me but leave that bag!"*

*Thieves thought, there certainly should be some valuable things in it.
They opened the bag and saw nothing but a bunch of blacked papers.
Thieves asked him: "What are these and what are they good for?"*

*"They are not of value to you but to me." Al-Ghazali replied.
And the conversation continued:*

"What kind of value?"

*"They are the result of years of striving and my education.
If you take them from me, all my knowledge acquired
through many years would be wasted and spoiled!"*

"Are they really your knowledge and wisdom?"

"Yes."

*Then one of them said:
"The knowledge that can be placed in a bag, carried and stolen,
is not the knowledge. Go and do something about yourself!"*

*These words from thieves shook Al-Ghazali and had
an impressive effect on his life afterward.*

Later, when Al-Ghazali had become a famous Master, he said:

*"The best advice given to me, guiding my
spiritual life was given by a bandit."*

The cognition is obtained in two ways, one is originated from the logic mind and deals with the how to do of an already known matter, or another type, which is the divine form of axioms related to much vaster dimension. Much beyond the dialectics!

The latter form is the part which is obtained by the man individually. The true wisdom allows Seeker deciding what to do and where to go, this is the means for communication between man and divinity and eventually their attendance.

The abundance of wisdom is by expanding one's knowledge.

The products of logic mind are limited and temporary while the universal wisdom related to the essence is eternal.

The logic mind cares for the easiest and most comfortable way available toward a certain goal, the divine mind although might be adventurous or risky in the eye of dialectics and contemporary lifestyle, yet it is the most effective and advantageous part to make one move forward in life!

The divine axiom requires more involvement from body and heart, thus making it more difficult to access and practice. Patience is the secret my friend!

Words

"Once in far distance, a talker man met his wise
neighbor. He went to him and said:
"Listen, I want to tell you a story about one of the
friends who was just talking about you…"

The wise neighbor interrupted him:
"Before you continue, tell me whether you have
Triple-filtered your language?"

"What is the triple-filter?"

"The first is the reality filter, are you sure
what you are going to say is true?"

"No…I just have heard it from someone." Man said.

The Wise man shook his hand surprisingly and added:
"Then for sure, you have passed it through happiness, the second
filter? If it is not true whether it is going to make me happy,?"

"I disappoint you that is not going to make you happy." Man said.

"Alright, if it does not make me happy, then it certainly has passed through the third filter which is "Gain filter". Is there any usefulness and benefit to me from what you are going to say?" The Wiseman asked.

"Not at all!" the talker said quietly.

The Wiseman continues:
"So, if it neither is true and not making me happy, nor of any use, in that case, keep it to yourself and try to forget it as soon as possible too!"

Certainly, the way of growth and development of man is gradual. From body to soul, from the root of the essence to the fruit of element, and by the combination of elements further, from insensibility to sensibility and eventually to become awakened, the process of perfection!

Some say, the man's soul, which is imprisoned in the body, has passed multitude worlds within thousands of years and it will pass many other worlds as well, with simple elements toward plants, animals and eventually man is passing through into last upheaval.

Seeker only remembers his death ambushing nearby and carries on my friend!

Love is the force behind all in the celestial sphere.

Observe your language, you are talking exactly about the deficit which your individual needs to work on for his development!

If words *only* would have been the reason of acquaintance, the dog would not be man's best friend!

Keep the words simple.

The true impressions are formed regardless of the complexity of the words and the length of speech.

Every word has a single meaning unless charlatanism is involved, directly or indirectly to make it more digestible, or for an ego's benefit. The best way of its expression is *Silence*!

For Seeker, words can be used when the right meaning is experienced!

The Quietude

"Get used to silence, Sometimes a sentence is enough to spoil it all,
Lucky is the one whose heart is connected to the eternity's one!

Sit silently in deep quietude, until you become speechless, effortlessly!

The quietude is the sign of present people."

Sheykh Bahaee, the Master

To become an observer, quietude is the condition to stick on. Persistence, Practice and Patience are the mysteries my friend!

Silence is the entry gate to the higher dimensions.

Prayer and meditations are doors toward the quietude.
Ceasing the conversation inside needs not to be in a special position at rest; however at the contemporary atmosphere of restlessness, it is performed more acceptably initially in such way to stop one from continuous competition!
Meditation is not to create a pleasant semi-conscious state and rest, but to be fully aware, knowing the self and the world and going

beyond continuously. After experiencing few glances of the quietude, Seeker gradually integrates silence to his activities.

This is a slow and solid process to be learned and applied. Patience and discipline are the secrets my friend!

Terminate the within conversation to see beyond the reach! Simultaneously, allow the physical body becomes aware of itself and function spontaneously by its own inbuilt intelligence.

The heart requires being involved fully in the self-development, hence flourishing the insight.

Allow the heart to be the observer.

The Piety

Bayazid Bastami, the great Sufi Master was asked:
"How did you achieve such high rank?"

The Master said as follow:
"One night my mother asked me for some water to drink.

I looked for it, there was no water in the house.
I took the jar and went toward the stream for water.

By the time I returned, she had already fallen asleep.
So, I thought: It will be wrong to wake her up.
Then I stood still holding the jar, making no noise,
and waited there for her to wake up."

At dawn, she woke up, looking at me and asked:
"Why are you standing there?"

I told her the story.

Then she prayed for me as follow:

"O Lord, make my son as dear to people, as he is dear to you!"

Conscious virtue causes advancement in the path and vice versa. But, Seeker prefers to proceed the path, hence virtue is the result and product, not the goal for him.

It's been said, remaining pious for forty consecutive days, opens the Eye of wisdom my friend!

Man is the focus of centers of various powers in existence. The differences between individuals are made by the measure of each power contributing in the centers and the amount of all powers involved in the centers. These powers are to be recognized and unfolded.

Sincerity and discipline are the requirements.

Resulting in consciousness expansion and true conscience formation.

These powers in contemporary era are being ignored and wasted by the ego. Once the piety is realized and put in action by Seeker, the consequences become obvious, thus the more purposeful actions and conducts are achieved progressively.

Initially, virtue appears as a cause of energy saving, but later it will be obvious that the virtue is result of this saving indeed!

The most common cause of energy waste is lust, ignorance, and ambition.

It requires a determined man my friend!

The expansion of consciousness with full presence is an efficient way to note the energy waste gates and thus correcting them.

Observing the actions attentively during eating, sex, anger, love, sadness, fear, disappointment, hope and all kind of other secret gestures and habits. Avoid repressing them, watch closely and reach to the central source of each action.

Observe the remorse contributing factors as well. Identify the provoking factors either externally or internally. The latter is the usual cause of all errors my friend!

Find also the social factors contributing in your individual actions, and correct them appropriately.

The Loneliness

"Deep in silence, there is a voice! To sense it, you need a heart!"

Shams, the Master

There is a unique path for every single man. This uniqueness forms the loneliness of individual. Loneliness is not a negative or unpleasant event, but the truth!

Although people live side by side, yet man is alone if present enough to note that! Every one is the owner and the creator of hers/his world.

There are friends to help, but the only one helping and keep one going forward efficiently, is you!

Friendship for being helped is beggary and trade! The real friendship comes from the heart, my friend!

That is why the self-recognition is the power and prerequisite.

And the sense of loneliness is eventually perceived, usually, as a sudden event.

Here, the sense of great responsibility and burden toward the self, others and the world with compassion forms.

Allow your heart to be the leader my friend!

It is one of the points where obstacles and hardships appear, but the advancement of Seeker in the path also greatly precipitates, resulting in transcendence. If one remains a sincere and compassionate observer enough, in harmony and present.

It is the point where one might sight sheep and wolves.

There is no need to be alone physically to feel the loneliness. This feeling is neither pleasant nor hard.

After this point, the process of self-realization enormously advances. And one will be able to find the deficits within, requiring attention.

The Insight

Some say, He created the Mind and told him:

"Get up…. Got up, the Mind.
Sit down…. Sat down, the Mind.
Come …. Went there, the Mind.
See…. Saw, the Mind."

And He said: "Oath to my dignity and glory, you
are my most honorable and dearest creation."

Then emerged selfishness in the Mind, of such caress and appeasement.

And the Creator Mighty said: "O Mind, look Thou back and sight!"

The Mind looked and saw a more pleasant face
and a worthier comeliness than his!

"Who are you? "The Mind asked.

And he said:

"I am the one, thee are useless without!

I am the Gracefulness!"

Dive courageously into the deep ocean and allow the heart to be present my friend!

The deeper one goes, the more mysterious it becomes, and by tasting the glimpses of truth, the mind becomes aware of its limits and learns to be quiet.

Confronting with the truth ascertains the vulnerability and inability of the man beside all his capabilities. This occurs in the vacuum produced by the inability of logic mind to confront the reality.

One might feel absurdity with demotivating effect, disappointment, or confusion.

Trust, Love, Discipline, and Acceptance are the keys!

Moving toward the essence requires confronting with all situations, good or evil! Lay away the judgeship my friend!

"Insight" is developed in such way as a never-ending process. But this should not be achieved purposefully by Seeker.

The boundaries of different worlds are realized here.

Remaining the observer constantly will allow comprehension of diverse patterns.

The deeper insight is, the more complete the patterns become!

On the Body

Long time ago, there were two friends, traveling together, one
of them was looking weak, having a meal once every other
night, and the other was strong, having three meals a day.

By misfortune, nearby a city, they were
arrested on charges of espionage.
They were left in a remote house with all doors
and windows locked and blocked to die.
Two weeks later, however, they were proved to be innocents,
and guards were sent to the remote house and free them,
if still alive. When they opened the doors, surprisingly,
found the strong man dead, but the weak man alive!

A Wise Physician concluded:
"I would have been surprised if the weak one has died indeed!
Death of the strong man was caused by overeating
and he could not survive the fourteen days battle.
While the weak man abstaining as usual,
Patiently survived."

Seventy percent of the physical body is made of Water. The question arises whether we contain it, or water contains *us* my friend!

Properties of water are contained in you as well. The body's unique physical properties, texture, and consistency are mostly because of the certain amount of water contained in it. Water is clear and transparent. One can see through it. Sincere and calm.

It reaches to the deepest and untouchable places on earth efficiently, easily, with no expectation, quite down to earth.

It cuts through solid rocks to find its way with patience and quietly. But that is not a goal for water! Flexibility and Patience are its mysteries my friend!

Be formless as water, become solid when necessary and vaporize to purify, to depart, to fly, but remember the self. It is the Flexibility!

Water vaporizes to lighten and to purify. This is the Purification!

Water gives life to all generously and uniformly. That is the sincerity!

All animate on earth contain water. Pure water from the springs moves down toward the ocean.

Imagine the task for man is to reverse this process to the peak and gain its purity back.

Water is a solvent. The more condensed and accumulated a man is, the less vibrant and conscious he becomes. Water is wise my friend!

Eat correctly and consciously to keep the body healthy. Listen to your body!

Have you ever tried a long fast challenge?

Self-Awareness

"The rectitude of work, where?! And I ruined
wanting in rectitude, where!
Behold the distance of the Path, from where rectitude to ruin, where!

With profligacy the being severed from friend and stranger;
what connection have rectitude and piety hypocrisy?

The hearing of the exhortation that affects not the heart where?!
The melody of the stringed instrument of Master, where!

My heart wearied of the cloister, and of the
patched garment of hypocrisy.

The Magians' cloister the circle of the Master where?!
The pure wine of the love of Creator where!"

Hafez, the Tongue of Mystery,

The sensation of Self is complex and limited to express by worlds and language.

It can be sensed in any location inside or outside the physical body.

The act of possession partially produces the sense of self, yet, it is the awareness, playing the major role in this peculiarity my friend!

By persistent practice and compassionate discipline, its size amplifies.

By gradual growth, it moves toward the unity of self and non-self.

The only compassionate and honest self-sensation would result in uniform and righteous union of within and without, befitting the Seeker!

In the perfection way of self-awareness, there is a point that cannot be missed, and that is where one obviously sights the border of within and without, where the physical body become a dust in the air!

It is not a goal! One becomes aware of it only following its achievement.

These days "to be", requires becoming my friend!

The Forgiveness

"I have no thought, but of Thee!
There is no more beautiful thought in any head, but of Thee!

There are dangers in the path of love, although...
But nil to affect the Man in love of Thee!"

Salman Savoji, the Man of distinction, the Poet

Imagine you are a long see-plant surrounded by many similar, moving and dancing with each other waving and whirling around, deep in the ocean.

If you prosper by silence gaining the wisdom of " the dance", it allows you to sight forces in play.

Surrender is the clue! Be a dancer, be present!

Seeker requires to see and move with an honest eye, and act wisely!

Forgiveness is a character of the man. Seeker walks very quietly, with his head down, as no one is there,

Yet fully aware of all around my friend!

The Treasure of Silence

Long ago, there was a man, trying to teach a donkey how to talk.
He was enforcing the poor donkey where through articulations, and
he was eagerly expecting imminent improvement in his work.
When a sage passing by, heard the story, went to him and said:
"Oh fool! Don't try in vain, otherwise, people start
blaming you for madness. Forget your false dream,
the donkey is not going to teach how to speak!

But, you can learn "Silence" from him if you are wise enough!"

Silence is further beyond usual mind's quietude, yet mind quietening is a pre-requisite for the silence.

To achieve the silence, one requires disabling five senses and wait for the heart guidance.

There is a source for all the situations and conditions and an ordinary man would be able to play one of them in its best shape in his life time, but he can be accessed to all of them by ceasing the inner talk, seeker requires first let his own condition go and then witness the rest with no bondage.

Advancing in meditation is an example. One requires to go

further and keep the mind quiet more during the day and night and while in daily activity.

The silence is beyond visual, acoustic, psychological inputs, and experiences.

Man is not a strong entity, nevertheless, it can be improved and strengthened in all aspects.

Witnessing of the self and surrounding, considering as much as the different point of views and angles toward dispersing in the ocean. It is a strong weapon available to man.

Patience is the secret my friend!

Self-Remembering

"O Saki (Tapster) forward, a cup of divine wine of the truths dash!
For, those sleep-stained, and wakeful of fortune.

In the musical note, what path is this that the minstrel struck?
That, togetherness, the Drunk and the Sober dance!

From this opium mystery that the Saki the master casteth into wine
To the rivals the Gnostics remaineth neither head nor
turban… so intoxicated on hearing it, are they

Hafez, the Tongue of Mystery"

It requires higher energetic range to remember one self, continuously.

Man's body is being replaced completely at regular intervals, throughout the life. The degree of self-awareness creates the presence, witnessing the fire inside or the essence.

Logic is a limiting factor my friend!

It is an inducible phenomenon in others, animals, and all other objects.

All states of being are transient, if pleasant sooner or later the sense to be resistant and dull, and if unpleasant as well to be overcome and faded away. Leave them all and remain the observer.

Remembering is a capability and property of all creatures and in man, highly complex and sophisticated form of it. In the contemporary, self-remembering is at its basic level and shallow, simply just to keep one alive in most comfortable way.

Enthusiastic practice expands self-remembering in true meaning.

To accelerate the presence, unlearning and freeing the slots are requisites, and gradually beginning to use the slots with a deeper insight compassionately, yet remembering that the slots are to be used temporarily and freed regularly.

This process is to expand the consciousness leading to self-recognition.

Forgetting at the surface level, is passive and supported by close external vicinity's stimuli and remembering is an active process requiring higher energetic range for its development.

Try every night to remember all the events done throughout the day in a reverse time mode of view, beginning from the most recent, and moving back toward the first things done in the morning.

Remember full events, details are not as important as realizing the occurrences of the facts.

Discipline is the key and love is the authority my friend!

It requires self-presence memoir and practicing own knowledge to expand the field and guide the path.

Note your emotions and their causes and origins, watch your body attentively.

Watch these communications impartially!

The Beyond

"The one, having a 'Need' in the Kharabat-corner;*
Drunk or Sober, his prayers will be answered!

Today, there won't accept any expedient nor diets;
The sole res there to be accepted of thee, the ' your Need' is,

No one knows the mysteries of the Kharabat, but the drunk;
How can the Sober know the mystery of this dwelling?"

Fakhr-al-Din Iraqi
The Master, the Poet

The beyond is out of reach. It requires senses out of this world to see, not the ones on the face!

Gratitude and surrender are the clues.

By striving one may reach to its border and notice the coast, to enter the ocean. A courageous heart is required!

Beyond cannot be a goal my friend. It is always there and that is you who need to explore it!

---

* *Kharabat: Tavern-House*

Are you sure that you have the capacity to face the truth? To find the answer, it is enough to contemplate and see yourself and the truth.

To expand the capacity, one requires transferring all the contents to a buffer zone, where they can be easily and readily evacuated with minimal un-necessary hooking to them.

By appropriate self-recognition and establishing a way of communication, further gain and support for Seeker onward will be achieved.

True dreaming is a little flick of beyond taste. One should not be sleeping to dream my friend!

By advancing the way, the sporadicity of true dreams turns to the perpetual manner of experience.

Have you ever attempted "conscious entrance" to the sleep and dream?

The Dilemma

A disciple of a great master asked him at the master's deathbed:
"Who was your master my dearest?"

-"I have had hundreds of them."

-"Which one was the most influential to you?"

The master thought and said:
"In fact, the most important truths were
inducted to me by three of them.
My first master was a Thief.
On one occasion, I reached home late at night and did not have
my keys with me, and I did not want to wake others up.
I met a man, asking him for help, and he easily in a glance opened
the door. I was amazed and asked him to teach me that.
He said that he is a thief and his job is to steal.
I invited him to stay overnight. He stayed with me for a month.
He used to go out every night and when he was back, used to
say, "I haven't got anything. I will try again tomorrow."
He was very pleased, I never saw him depressed and failed.

The second was a dog coming to a river daily to quench his thirst, but as soon as by the river, he would see another dog in the water, he was scared and pulled back immediately. Eventually, to kill the extreme thirst, one day, he decided to confront the obstacle and threw himself into the water, and concurrently, the image of the dog was also vanished!

My third master was a little girl passing in the street by a bright-lighted candle.
I asked her.
-"Did you turn on the candle yourself?"

-"Yes." She answered.

To teach her a lesson, I said:
-"My dear, where did the flame come from before you turned it on?"

The little girl laughed, turned the candle off, asking me:
"Can you tell me where the flame's just gone??"

Then I realized just like that candle, there is a sacred flame inside the heart available in certain moments, but one never knows, how to turn it on, or where it comes from!"

When Seeker becomes familiarized with the path, when he notes the common implements keeping the man in the way or deviating him out of it, he gradually begins to stabilize.

There is a dilemma in the path to confront my friend!

Although it might show up in early stages initially, but it will disappear and returns finally on the right time.

Unless there is a battle inside, keeping the fire alive, man is present, otherwise, he is in deep sleep and unaware. The battle is between the mind and heart. Stay an Observer regardless of whichever appears right!

The love and conscience are the keys to keep the flame alive!

The relation between the master and disciple is only a story outside appearing, Note the love and unity behind the veil.

This is the property of battle inside, keeping you looking after the other option, regardless of their natures.

Man requires to mature in all aspect to confront with the dilemma.

Fame and name, or "none"?

There is never a mark of rightness and wrongness to either side of equations in these two questions.

Allow the body and heart maneuvering and experiencing their wishes and explore the world and share the information together.

Be and behave as an individual toward others. Note their presence simultaneously as yours.

Prepare your body, mind and heart my friend!

Nature

In distance time, there were two friends, a Mystic and a Darvish. The Mystic was a wealthy man, while the Darvish's only property was his famous cup, "the Kashkool". The Darvish used to emphasize his piety through his poverty. One day, Darvish was guest of his friend, and to remind his austerity again, asked his friend whether he would leave all his belongings and wealth, going with him to a remote temple to worship?

-"Of course… Let's go there right now!": The Mystic replied.

-"I'm not sure how long it might take. Are you going to leave your wealth and castle behind?" Darvish asked surprisingly and unbelievably.

-"Yes, if you are ready, let's go." The Mystic said.

Soon after they began the journey, suddenly on the way, Darvish said:
-"Oh dear, I've left my Kashkool!"

And the Mystic said:

> *-"My friend, you still have attachments to give up! Having*
> *is not a hinderence! The wealthier, the better,*
> *The labor is to let go!"*

We all belong to nature. The way toward individuality and higher freedom platform require unifying self with nature.

Live as natural and as simple as possible my friend!

Be speechless while communicating with nature. Allow your heart to communicate.

Feel the alertness and the presence, yet full of harmony and love.

Feel the entities in nature. Feel the powers. Touch and unite with them compassionately. You are the most sophisticated product of nature! Remember to represent them all below hands as well!

True Morality

There was a famous Master sitting by stream and crying.

*Watching the situation, the disciples soon began
to worry and one of them asked him:
"What is the matter, Master? Whether
someone has told you something?"*

*The Master said among the cries:
-"Yes, one of the villains around told me
something which is disturbing me!"*

-"What did he say?" Disciples asked anxiously.

*-"He told me, I am truly the one, that people
talk about;*

*O Master,
Are you truly the one, people are talking about too?!*

*This is the question, making me
think strange since!"*

True morality is deep and complex. It is not the law yet arranging in supreme.

The true morality is experienced, and it becomes the character of Seeker, there is no requirement to search for it. It will gradually be expressed in right time and place through him.

True morality is not an instruction for righteousness but rather the outcome of it. It is formed in the way toward individuality.

Respectfulness, in a true sense appearing from the heart is the key!

It considers the true and full value of non-judgmental observation and witnessing.

Try to be respectful sincerely to yourself and the outside world.

True knowledge and wisdom help to familiarize with respectfulness in an appropriate manner.

It requires to consider depth in full sense for all and realize the dimensions beyond.

Courage

"If Thou don't know the art of colors in the field of flowers,
Don't call them ugly, nor beauteous!

To see by heart… That is
The Man's way!

Don't look for the flaws in others!

Rumi, the Master, the Poet"

Courage is a heart's venture for all actions of Seeker.
But what is courageous to one might not be to another my friend!

Real courage is expressed when true morality is developed.
It requires confronting with difficult situations.

Desirelessness

At times far away, there was a poor Peasant, surviving hardly,
until one year he lost all his crops due to drought, where he
decided to travel and make some change in his living situation.

Soon in his journey, after a while, he reached to a large forest.
While entering it, he noted a white bearded man sitting quietly on
a huge rock. He decided to go forth and gather some information.

Having said his story, asked for some advice.

The white bearded man said:
"If you go toward South in the forest, when you reach
the river, on your right, there are long trees with quality
woods. You might sell them and use the money"

The Peasant thanked him and went there and cut the woods
and he made a good sum of money to live for a year, when he
returned back to the same forest to continue his journey.
He noted the white bearded man again on the same rock.
And he asked for the same advice.

*"If you keep going for a half a day, toward East
from the river onward, there is a small green hill
which if you dig there is a copper mine there.*

*The Peasant thanked him again and went there,
he dug and established the copper mine and he was
living in a blissful way for three more years.
The mine was completely used and again the Peasant returned
to the forest and met the whitebeard man again.*

*"There is a huge old fig tree near the lake toward North which
if you dig, beneath it there is an old gold treasure...*

*The Peasant interrupted him:
"Wait! You know all about these goodies and secrets,
why you are not going there yourself?!"*

*The Master looked at him quietly and said:
"It takes a long time to reach to this point where I am sitting now!"*

By maturing the true self, man can see the fuel being used by the mind to keep tossing in the world of desires.

Being desire free does not mean being in a wandering state, but full presence.

It is achieving the state of no need to have a desire to live.

It means all the known states are experienced and Seeker remains seeking. Good or evil, are finished. The *surrendering* is the outcome my friend!

Man is living in a river of desires and it is impossible to stay there and not to get wet! However, by staying conscious and by having a strategy, one can minimalize the effects by the river. And eventually notice beyond the ordinary world.

At the end, all desires become unified to one, which is the character of the religious man, and finally the realization of desirelessness.

Surrender to truth is the clue!

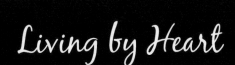

Living by Heart

A beloved asked her lover to join her in the house.
The lover pulled out several heart-rending letters from his pocket, he
used to write while away from the beloved and started to read them.
The letters were full of sighs and whining.
Soon after reading few letters, the beloved was bored
and said with a look of ridicule and humiliation:
-"Whom have you written these letters for?"

-"For you, sweetheart."

The beloved said: "I am present here and sitting by
you and you may enjoy the presence and togetherness.
What you do, is just a waste of life and of time."

The lover replied:
"True! I am aware of it, but I wonder why I still enjoy your thoughts
and memories when even being alone and away from you!"

The beloved added: "You love your states, not me! I am like
the house and the position of the beloved and not beloved
body. You are dependent on your own states. The true lover
settles timelessly and formlessly. The true lover is the kinglet
of all states and you are captive of your own states!

You go and learn "how to love" from the true lovers!
Otherwise, you remain the slave."
Forget your beauty and ugliness, but the love!
But the beloved! Liberate your weakness and power.
But the lofty and determined efforts.
And always in the search of it.

From Masnavi, By Rumi, the Master, the Poet

The quantity of heart present in man is additive. It expands by time and space.

The heart quantity is measurable. One might distinguish its border, where a contact arises between the personality and the individuality of self. This contact is experienced by self through various feeling.

In this zone is also where social laws are written and norm is manufactured. By observation of oneself and awareness, one can plan and witness its progression.

The heart quantity adds up to individuality, and one can expand the individuality by noting the complex acts occurring in this border and those arose purely from heart might be accepted by one's true-being, hence the heart measure, is added up to the individuality.

Honesty and love are the mysteries!

By working on them and living more with one's true self this border gets recognized and is moved further beyond. In this way, the circle expands continuously.

In this way, one dissolves in what is being done.

Living by heart with a full sense of love, joy, braveness, honesty, and presence continuously would be an appropriate way to keep one in the path. The rest would adjust itself to this core to guide you toward it and toward the essence and beyond.

I pray that for you my friend!

The art of Forgetting

"Such a one am I that the Kharabat — corner, is the cloister of mine.
The prayer from the Master of wine-sellers is the morning task of mine.
Although the melody of the harp of the
morning be not mine, what fear?

At morning time there is insurrection my
cry, is the excuse utterer of mine.
Of the king and the beggar, I am free.
Thanks, God be praised!

The beggar of the dust of the Friend's door is king of mine!

Hafez, the Tongue of Mystery"

Forget everything but yourself, my friend!

Forgetting is a complex phenomenon of unlearning, minimizing
the effect or inactivating of learned matters or their effects.
Forgetting passively occurs directly by the removal
of external forces producing the action of man.

Forgetting actively requires effort and energy
and it is usually by minimizing the effect or
inactivating the previously learned subject.

By forgetting, initially, spaces become available for
further self-development and expansion.
Purposeful saving and directing the internal
energy is required for the process.
The further one goes ahead on the path the more
complex and deeper habits of different nature will
appear from deep within. They require unlearning!
Self-purification is also part of the forgetting.

Knowledge is held mostly by the mind. It causes knowledgeability.
Avoiding knowledgeability is the art of forgetting.

For the expansion of consciousness, it requires
both to add up true knowledge and uncover the
unknown and by freeing the spaces occupied.
Forgiveness is the art of forgetting!
Detachment is the forgetting!
Graciousness is also the art of forgetting!

Try by close observation and by the bits of advice given by near
ones, find your habits and correct them deeply from the roots.
Forget all habits, pleasant or none.

All man knows is not absolute, but his
perception, understanding from without.
Let it go my friend!

And, one day, you wake up fully aware and present
of your true self in your own journey.

Forget the words and writings my friend!

This too shall pass!

Printed in the United States
By Bookmasters